HEALING YOUR HEART

Healing Your Heart

LAUREN MILO

CONTENTS

Forward

Dear Reader,

Welcome to the 90 Day Heal Your Heart Challenge. What began as a personal challenge of learning how to love myself has evolved into a community of people seeking a deeper understanding of their own hearts and how they can cultivate self-love and care.

Enclosed in this book are days one through thirty of the challenge. Each day has a unique journal prompt or exercise designed to bring you deeper into awareness with yourself and your heart. My hope is that at the end of the challenge you will have three beautiful books that encapsulate how you healed your heart. In essence, you will have created a guidebook to your own love which can continue to be a source of comfort and reference as you move through life and love in their many stages.

The daily prompts follow the same order as the videos I've previously posted to TikTok and Instagram. I invite you to use those videos as an additional resource as you navigate your own journey. If you have any questions or insights you would like to share, I can be reached by direct message on TikTok and Instagram @lostgirltherapy.

Be well and be strong, your heart can't wait to hear from you.

Best,
Lost Girl Therapy

~ 1 ~

DAY 1: WHO TAKES CARE OF
YOUR HEART

Let's explore who takes care of your heart. Today, please review who has taken care of your heart in the past. I would begin by going back to childhood- who do you include in the group of people who showed you love, care and affection? How did their love shape the way you perceive and internalize love in your present life? If it is helpful, you can lay this out like a timeline marking who came into your life and when. With each mark on the timeline, I would add a "how they loved me" note.

For instance, if your grandmother came into your life the day you were born - say June 1, 1985 and she loved you through understanding and total acceptance you would have the following noted: Grandma, 6/1/1985, understanding and acceptance. After you have completed the timeline with everyone you would like to include, go back and review what pattern of love feels most significant to you. Do most people in your life offer you love that is demonstrated through understanding or maybe you feel most loved by those who demonstrate love with action. When you have seen how you are loved, reflect on what their love has done for you and contemplate if you offer your own heart the same type of love, recognition and understanding.

~ 1 ~

~ 2 ~

DAY 2: WHERE DOES YOUR MIND DRIFT

The mind has a brilliant mechanism for calling forward times of significance when it comes to the heart. It's a comforting thing to recall how we have participated in the act of love. On day two of this journey I invite you to explore your relationship with love and what narratives you have carried throughout life. When you think about loving someone or being loved where or to whom does your mind go? Does it go to a time where you loved someone else deeply or a specific person who taught you a new way to feel loved? Which direction your mind drifts to is an indicator of how you conceptualize love and how you've learned to be loved. Spend a few moments today jotting down the significant people or times in your life that stand out. Why are they significant to you? This is not a process of justification. This is a day to take note of who and what led you to this journey.

~ 3 ~

DAY 3: ABANDONING OUR HEARTS

For today's journal, I want you to think back to the first time you abandoned your heart. When I say abandonment, I mean the first time you thought someone else's heart was more worthy of receiving love than your own. Was it when you had your first crush or first relationship? Did it happen from a young age when you learned how to pay more attention to others than you did to yourself in order to fit in? The act of abandoning our hearts does not always tie to romantic interest so be mindful of also reviewing friendship and other significant relationships that may have prompted you to think less of yourself or put others in a higher regard when it came to love

~ 4 ~

DAY 4: HOW DO YOU FEEL WITHOUT YOUR HEART

This prompt is challenging, I'm not going to lie. It's challenging because it forces us to confront the result of our actions. When we give our heart away to others and we leave it out in the abyss or in the care of someone else, there is a direct result that occurs. Now what that is is up to you to determine. So today, I want you to think back to a time where you felt like you gave your heart away and what was the result? Try not to think of the results in the mindset of how someone else took care of your heart. Instead, turn inward and reflect on how you felt when your heart was in someone else's hands. Did you feel more nervous and concerned? Did you feel empty or achy? Did you feel an unexplainable yearning to be near them? Today we are intentionally calling forward the sensation of awareness when it comes to your heart by recognizing how you physically, mentally and emotionally process when your heart has left your space.

~ 5 ~

DAY 5: WHAT HAPPENS IF I LOVE MYSELF

Today, I want you to make a list of all the fears you carry about potentially loving yourself. What's the worst case your mind runs to if you continue on this journey? Perhaps you fear the way another loves you will be impacted or you fear stepping away from a love that hasn't served you but feels familiar. Today is a day of sitting in the uncomfortable and challenging the anxious mind to articulate effectively what it fears as it begins to reunite with your heart.

~ 6 ~

DAY 6: UNDERESTIMATING THIS

The art of learning how to heal your heart is not easy. If it was easy, everyone would learn how to love themselves before we learned how to love others. But that's not really the case too often is it? This is the work that challenges us to dismantle all of our limiting self-beliefs and negative self-concepts. This is the work that reignites our hearts and welcomes them back into the fold of the higher alignment between you and yourself. So today, let's take a moment to simply recognize that this is not easy but it is worth it. Allow yourself to sit in the space of understanding and knowing. During a moment of intentional reflection, feel the changes in yourself from day one to day six and notice if you feel or think differently. This is a day of recognition so give yourself time to feel the work within you and how it emanates out. I invite you consider processing in a way that is authentic to you so if quiet reflection doesn't feel aligned, consider an act that typically helps you process emotions such as a long walk or listening to music and allow the mind to flow.

~ 7 ~

DAY 7: REALIGNING THE ANXIOUS MIND

How do we re-learn how to listen to our heart's unique language? First we have to learn what it looks like when our anxious mind begins to worry about and interfere with our heart's work. On day seven of this journey you might begin to see that the anxious mind has begun encouraging you to stay in the space of familiarity. It might be saying, "this work is too hard, we cannot achieve it. Let's just keep doing what we're doing."

If that is what's happening, here is how we dismantle it: we go back to our souls. The exercise for today is learning how to cue your soul when you're anxious mind kicks up. Each time you feel a thought pass through the mind that says "I can't, I won't, we're not going to be able to do this" I want you to ask your soul what it feels to be right and true for you. Drop down to the space behind your belly button where deeper inner knowing or gut feelings exist and ask your soul if it agrees with the mind. The reason you are intentionally cueing the soul is because the anxious mind only has authority if the soul remains silenced. So today, we are bringing the soul to the forefront. The more you cue your soul, the quieter the mind gets, allowing you to hear your heart's language with greater clarity each day.

~ 8 ~

DAY 8: HEART DEPRIVATION

Your heart aches for something and if you don't give your heart what it needs, it has to go outside of you to find it. When we don't give our hearts love, they learn to go and seek it from others. The more we deprive our own hearts, the more willing our hearts are to accept any version of love from others even if it's poor quality or poor treatment. The greater the deprivation, the greater the need for fulfillment.

So for today, let us examine where we first learned how to deprive our hearts. Think about where you learned about the concept of romantic love and how you were taught to attain it. Did you think you had to make yourself less than or change your personality in order to be attractive to others? Did you ignore your heart's wants and needs and replace them with fulfilling the needs of others? Did you teach your heart to be in second place to someone else's? Reflect on the narratives you have and keep a journal about how this narrative impacted your romantic history. Notice how deprivation plays a role in how you view yourself in partnership and how deprivation shaped your concept of self-worth.

DAY 9: CRITICIZING OUR HEARTS JOB

We criticize ourselves so much that sometimes we forget we're even doing it. Part of this challenge is to stop the stem of criticism our hearts receive and challenge ourselves to embrace a new version of self-talk. Today, I invite you to journal on what you feel is your heart's job. What is your heart meant to do? Is it meant to keep you alive both physically and creatively? Is it meant to love someone else? Is it meant to be warm and comfortable and welcoming? When we become aware of what we want our heart's job to be we also become aware of how we've criticized it in the past. Be mindful and reflect on areas of your life when your heart fulfilled its job but you told it to do less or be less. Review your heartbreaks or the times you felt like your heart hurt too much. Did your heart receive the message that it needed to tone it down or change the way it showed up? Today is about re-establishing the relationship between you and your heart and in order to do that, we have to take accountability for our side of this equation through recognition and understanding of how we may have been criticizing our heart's job all this time.

~ 10 ~

DAY 10: THE DECISION MAKING CHECKLIST

This is one of my favorite days in this challenge so far. We are exploring what the mind says, the heart feels and the soul does when presented with something you want. The decision making checklist is the embodiment of integration between the soul, body, heart and mind. It is here that we learn to attune more fully into our signals and read them with a greater sense of accuracy. For this to work you have to have an understanding of your gut instinct aka your soul. If you do not have a full sense of understanding, I invite you to practice the art of intuition building (see day 7).

If you are comfortable with differentiating between the soul, heart and mind, begin by putting yourself into a space of quiet meditation. Visualize something or someone that you want and move the image up to your third eye (around the forehead or behind the eyes). Ask your mind "Do I want this?" and wait for an answer. When you've received one, move down to your heart.

You can put your heart in the chair across from you and invite what you want to sit next to it or you can simply focus on your heart chakra. Bring the original visualization down to your heart's level and ask your heart "Does this feel good?" Notice changes in this physical body in this space. The heart space is a beautiful area of attunement and changes to the chakra will be very present if you tune in well.

Finally, take your visualization and drop it down to your soul (around belly button level). In this space, I want you to take a moment and allow your soul to sit in the energy with this potential outcome. Allow your soul to explore what it would be like to be with that person or achieving that goal and then ask your soul "Does this feel right and good?" The soul tends to operate in a space of high clarity so you may find it's either a strong yes or a strong no. It can be helpful to visualize the soul like a balloon. When something is a yes (for me) it expands fully. When it's a no, I feel like the balloon deflate and almost a tiny gut punch.

The goal of this exercise is to attune to the mind, body and soul in order to gain clarity. When something is aligned on all three levels (whether it is a yes or no), you will soon see and feel the difference between acting on it or not. When there is a lack of clarity (say the soul and mind don't agree and the heart feels torn), explore identifying where the disagreement lies by using curious questioning with yourself or journaling on the feelings that arise from the disagreement.

~ 11 ~

DAY 11: GRANTING PERMISSION
TO YOUR HEART

Some modern narratives around love teach us that we need to give our heart away in order to be loved. So let's flip the script. Instead of giving our heart away, let us become selective of who we all to access it. Our heart's capacity for love is boundless so it is up to us as guardians of our hearts to be mindful of who we allow permission to when it comes to receiving our love. Today I want you to reflect on the concept of granting permission. What type of requirements would someone need to meet in order to access a piece of your heart? Do they need to demonstrate trust? Do they need to have a high sense of integrity? Whatever your requirements are, document them and be specific. If it's helpful to take some time away to process, do so and then come back and refine what requirements your heart holds.

~ 12 ~

DAY 12: WHAT DOES YOUR HEART HEAR?

How do you speak to your heart? Your heart does many jobs and perhaps we are not thanking it enough for all it does. How do you respond when your heart hurts or when it feels love? Do you chastise it for getting itself broken if you love and it doesn't work out? Do you tell your heart to not get ahead of itself when you meet someone you really like? Pay attention to how you speak to your heart when it tries to connect with you or with someone else. Take time today to journal on how the language you've chosen for your heart affects the job your heart is meant to do: love and be loved.

~ 13 ~

DAY 13: GOING BACK TO RECLAIM THE PAST

We're going down memory lane folks. But not in the way you think. I want you to review past times you've felt loved or people that you've loved and ask yourself what parts of you did you leave in those situations? What parts of you, your soul and your heart got left behind? When you've identified those parts, I want you to ask yourself if those parts exists in your current life. If the answer is yes, evaluate how they show up and where the show up most fully. If the answer is no, ask yourself how you can reintegrate those parts of you back into your present moment and what actions it will take for you to do so. Be mindful that this is not a prompt about opening up old wounds or calling forward past relationships. This is about *you* reclaiming the parts of you that got left behind.

~ 14 ~

DAY 14: WHAT ARE YOU LOOKING FOR IN LOVE

For today, ask yourself the following: What are you looking for in love? Before you jump into it (because I know you almost stopped reading)... add the second part of the question: What are you looking for in love from yourself? Of course you can begin by evaluating what you are looking for in love from others but if you start there, be mindful that what we seek in others can be what we feel we are missing in ourselves. So in this instance, if you find you are seeking something specific in love, inquire within yourself to see if it's also something you want when comes to self-love. For example, are you seeking to be understood? Are you seeking to be unconditionally loved? Are you seeking attention and comfort? At the end of the journal, I invite you take the things you're seeking and make them into a list beginning with "I am seeking..." In the future, you may come back to this list and find that all you've been seeking has been accomplished.

~ 15 ~

DAY 15: NO REGRETS WHEN IT COMES TO LOVE

On this day, make a list of those you've loved who didn't work out. Instead of asking yourself what regrets you have about them (please don't do that), ask yourself if you have any regrets about *how* you loved them. We cannot control others but when things don't work out it's easy to believe that it's because of how we tried to love someone. Today, reflect on how you loved each person and ask yourself if you have any regrets about how that love manifested the relationship. Pay special attention to not allow shame into the equation. This is not a shame exercise. This is about holding awareness for how you love others because how you love others clues us into how you can learn to love yourself.

~ 16 ~

DAY 16: YOU ARE YOUR GREATEST SOURCE OF KNOWLEDGE

On this day, I invite you to reflect on all the things you've learned about yourself over the years. Instead of listing accomplishments and accolades, dig deep. Think about what you've learned about who you are as a person. Pay attention to your physical health and your mental/emotional well-being. Have you gained a deeper understanding of how you operate? Do you feel like you understand the signals of your body and how they impact your emotions? Everything that occurs within us is trying to tell us something. Today, let's take a moment to see how well we've been listening.

DAY 17: WAITING ON SOMEONE ELSE

If you have a history of waiting for others to show up for you (don't we all), today is the day I want us to reflect on what that waiting has done. Think back to all the times you put your life on hold for someone else. Pay attention to the toll the waiting has taken on all areas of your life. Then reflect on times where you chose to stop waiting and step away, back to yourself. Notice how these moments feel different not only in the physical body but also in the mental and emotional realms.

~ 18 ~

DAY 18: WHEN YOUR HEART
FEELS DIFFERENT

Today I want you to tune into the sensation of your physical body. Throughout the day, reflect on how your heart feels when you think about things that impact you in a positive way. For example, how does your heart feel when you think about getting a great cup of coffee on the way to work? How does it feel when the sun is shining? Then pay attention to how your heart feels when your attention moves to someone or something else. This is particularly easy to notice if your attention often drifts to a love interest. Does your heart feel strong or does the space in your chest feel mildly empty? Do you notice a change in your heartbeat? Does your body language begin to shift? All of this information helps us become more aware of how our heart changes when we shift our attention away from it.

~ 19 ~

DAY 19: ANXIOUS ATTACHMENT?
BRING YOUR HEART HOME

If you are someone who identifies with being anxiously attached, I invite you to sit in a moment of quiet reflection. Feel your breath in your body. Feel your feet on the floor. When you feel a sense of calm I want you to visualize your heart in front of you. Place it in a chair across from you and simply sit in the sensation of quiet stillness. When you feel connected to it, place the first person that comes to mind in the chair next to your heart and see which direction your heart goes. Does it move closer to the other person? Does it stay grounded in its seat? No matter what your heart does – thank the person for showing you what you needed to know and allow them to disappear from the chair. Once you are back in the space with just you and your own heart, ask your heart if it would like to come home. Notice if your heart hesitates or it doesn't feel ready. That's okay. There's no necessity for it to come home in this moment. This meditation is about giving your heart the invitation to return to you when it feels ready. When your heart does feel ready to come home to you, visualize it moving closer to your heart chakra until it re-integrates within your physical body. Allow yourself time to reacclimate to your heart being back in its original place within you.

If you are someone who identifies with being avoidantly attached, I invite you to sit in a moment of quiet reflection. Feel your

37

breath in your body. Feel your feet on the floor. When you feel a sense of calm I want you to visualize your heart in front of you. Place it in a chair across from you and simply sit in the sensation of quiet stillness. Here, ask your heart where it has felt closed off. Perhaps go so far as to ask your heart who it wanted to love but didn't or couldn't. When your heart responds, try to sit in the space of compassion and understanding. For the avoidant heart, it's important to invite in warmth so try to focus on emotions that make you feel calm and serene. When you feel a sense of understanding between you and your heart, ask it what it needs more of.

If you are someone who identifies as disorganized/ fearful avoidant or securely attached, review the above exercises and try both. If you feel drawn to one more than the other, trust your intuition. Your soul and your heart work in tandem to show you what you need to know. Take a moment to trust them and see what you come away with.

~ 20 ~

DAY 20: YOU CAN TRY TO RUN FROM YOURSELF BUT...

I'm not going to lie – this is a challenging prompt. Because when we have learned how to avoid ourselves, the thought of facing our own hearts becomes that much more daunting. However, today I invite you to embrace your own fears and instead of wielding them into avoidant behavior, let us turn them into action. Make a list of times when you feel most eager to run from yourself. Ask yourself "Where do I go" and why? Pay attention to moments of self-sabotage or escapism, moments where the anxiety has felt too great so you find a way to release it that you later have second thoughts about. All of this recognition is not about introducing shame. It is about lifting the veil of fear and embracing the notion that you can hold all parts of yourself even in discomfort.

~ 21 ~

DAY 21: JOURNEY TO SELF-LOVE

What does your journey to today look like? Each of us has an experience of getting to the point of embracing our hearts and learning how to love ourselves. Your journey is unique and today is about documenting the path that got you here in order to honor, recognize and embrace all the wins, trip ups, and challenges along the way. I would advise beginning from the moment you feel most aligns with your first step into the self-development journey. I invite you sit in a space of quiet reflection and speak to your heart. Notice if it sounds or feels different. If you visualize your heart across from you, has it changed in color, shape and textured? Does it look and feel healthier? This day is about recognition of what change looks like when you pour love back into yourself.

DAY 22: CELEBRATING ACCOMPLISHMENTS

When it comes to accomplishments we could easily fall into the mindset of a running list of things we've done where we've received validation from others. But on this day, we're not worried about that. We are thinking about the moments in your life where you have felt proud of what you've done, who you are or how you've acted in past scenarios. Pay special attention to how you spoke to yourself in those moments. Was it with tenderness and love? Did you have a moment of basking in a sensation of pride? Regardless of how you acknowledged it previously, today I invite you to say "I am so proud of me" after each memory comes to the surface. Feel the warmth spread across your body and take note of the other sensations that arise.

~ 23 ~

DAY 23: HONOR THE WAY YOU LOVE

Consider how you love people in your life. Today, make a list of what it means for you to show love towards others. Think back to times where you showed care and deep understanding, where you showed up and where you held space. This practice of intentionally drawing attention to your heart's way of loving is to remind you that the way you love is unique to you and deserves recognition even if no one else is currently there to see it.

~ 24 ~

DAY 24: FINDING WHAT YOU
SEEK

Today I invite you to review where your heart goes when it wants to leave you. Pay attention to who you feel called to or what type of escapism you might be craving. When you've identified what those things are, think about what need those people or circumstances fulfill in you and challenge yourself to evaluate how you can fulfill that need within yourself.

~ 25 ~

DAY 25: THERE'S NO RUSH

Today let's talk about timelines. When it comes to healing the heart we can forget that timelines impact us whether or not we are consciously aware of it. I invite you to journal about how timelines have previously impacted how you felt about yourself whether in the heart space or in another area of your life. Do timelines make you feel like you're under pressure? Do they add the risk of disappointing others into the mix? When it comes to the heart, there is no set timeline for reconnecting with you with you. Today, consider what it would mean for you to free yourself of the timelines you carry and ask yourself how your heart would act and feel differently if you did.

~ 26 ~

DAY 26: WHAT'S YOUR NEW STANDARD?

Let's take a moment to evaluate what new standards of love we hold for our own hearts. Over the last twenty-six days, our hearts have redefined what they seek in love both from ourselves and from others. So today, take a moment to evaluate how your standards of love have evolved from the past. Review past romantic love, friendships and family relationships. Ask yourself how your love evolved, sustained or faded. What made it grow? What made it feel stifled? What helped you find greater clarity when it came to understanding what it is that makes you feel loved or perhaps, not loved in each moment of the past?

DAY 27: WHAT ARE YOU SEEKING IN LOVE?

It's natural to believe that this prompt encourages you to go back and review past loves. But if you jump too quickly to that conclusion you will miss out on its actual intention. For day twenty-seven I invite you to review your past relationships (romantic or otherwise) and recall what you were seeking out of the dynamic. Try not to fall into the trap of recalling what you wanted from the other person. Broaden your perspective and consider what you were seeking at that specific moment in time in general. When you have gained awareness for what you were seeking, see how you satisfied that need. Was your partner or friend able to fulfill it or were they unable to do so and you ended up fulfilling it yourself? Is the need still unfulfilled within you? By taking stock of what we are seeking both from the past and the present we're holding ourselves in a greater space of understanding for the journey we've taken thus far and the one we've yet to experience.

~ 28 ~

DAY 28: APPRECIATING
YOURSELF PART 1

The art of appreciating yourself is about fine tuning what it means to show yourself positive affirmation and support. Appreciating ourselves begins with recognition and celebration for how we love. On day twenty-eight, I invite you to evaluate what your favorite qualities of your heart are. Consider what you find to be the most pleasant and celebratory aspects of how your heart loves. Do you show up for others? Are you someone who always remembers a birthday? Are you known for having an endless amount of support for others? Take time today to write about your heart the way you would speak about your most cherished loved one and notice how your heart feels and responds differently when it feels appreciated by its first love.

~ 29 ~

DAY 29: APPRECIATING YOURSELF PART 2

Today, reflect back on times you have received appreciation from those around you especially about how you love. Notice how their feedback sits within your heart chakra. Does it feel gratifying because you agree with it? Does it fall short of what you expected it to feel like? Navigating your relationship with appreciation from others harkens back to seeking external praise so you may see similarities between how your heart feels in this moment and how your soul feels when you are externally validated. These moments are not meant to be changed, poked, prodded or diluted into something to make sense of. The goal of today's journal is simply awareness and recognition for how the heart responds when it's put in the position to be seen by others.

~ 30 ~

DAY 30: CLOSURE

Phew. You've made it. Congratulations on completing the first thirty days of the Heal Your Heart Challenge. Today, I invite you to complete any exercise that brings you closure. Closure from seeking love from others before we seek love from ourselves. Closure from all the moments we stepped away from our own hearts or abandoned them in the hopes of replacing them with someone else's. Closure from each time we dismissed the way we loved because it didn't feel like it was good enough based on other people's standards.

In whatever way feels right and good, I invite you to complete a closure exercise. Perhaps some moments of meditative silence to release old wounds or people. Maybe a journaling exercise recognizing how far you've come or calling a close friend to share your most recent insights and growth. Whatever route you choose, lead with the intention of releasing what no longer serves you and embracing what is yet to come.